RUDE
PUZZLE
BOOK

Naughty
Brain-Teasers
for Grown-
Ups

Richard Cox

summersdale

RUDE PUZZLE BOOK

An Hachette UK Company
www.hachette.co.uk

Summersdale Publishers Ltd
Part of Octopus Publishing Group Limited
Carmelite House
50 Victoria Embankment
LONDON
EC4Y 0DZ

www.summersdale.com

Printed and bound in China

ISBN: 978-1-78783-026-4

Substantial discounts on bulk quantities of Summersdale books are available to corporations, professional associations and other organizations. For details contact general enquiries: telephone: +44 (0) 1243 771107 or email: enquiries@summersdale.com.

INTRODUCTION

It's time to put down your phone, tablet or smutty magazine and pick up this crude collection of conundrums. And when we say "crude", we mean it! Whether you want to dive straight into the Bootylicious Bottoms Word Search, test your logic with a Raunchy Riddler, or even try your hand at the Sex Toys Sudoku, there are puzzles here to tickle a whole range of fancies and fill up those idle hours.

So, what are you waiting for? If you're a puzzle fanatic with a preference for the profane, then this is the book for you. Just remember to keep it tucked away from prying eyes if there are any small folk around!

TEASING TOYS CROSSWORD

Across

3 Related to Bilbo? (5)

6 Use this to push the boat out. (8, 6)

Down

1 If you like it then you should've put a ____ ____ on it. (4, 4)

2 This item doesn't go in the usual socket. (4, 4)

4 This toy will get you buzzing. (8)

5 Kinky is using the whole chicken, erotic is just the ____. (7)

MAZE

Can you help Leon find the kinkiest wristwear for his date this evening?

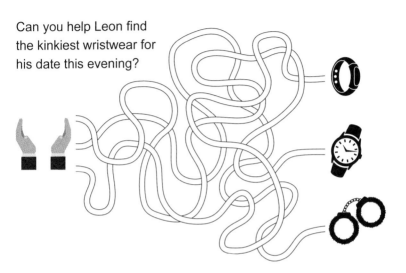

WORD LADDER

Change TOSS into BABE by altering one letter at a time to make a new word on each step of the ladder:

T O S S

— — — —

— — S —

— — — —

B A B E

DOT-TO-DOT

Join the dots to find the mystery image!

MISSING WORDS

Fill in the blank space to make two compound words or phrases:

Cock		Road
Smoking		Head
Balls		Throat
Landing		Tease

BEAUTIFUL BOOBIES WORD SEARCH

```
X  U  H  O  B  G  M  I  T  I  Y  J  R  M  E
T  E  Q  H  Z  S  X  F  O  H  T  S  M  S  X
H  K  U  X  K  P  E  N  B  I  W  S  Q  A  P
R  X  O  M  C  O  C  L  B  U  H  S  K  M  M
O  D  X  B  Q  Q  P  Z  C  K  E  G  F  O  X
S  A  G  N  A  H  C  I  M  I  H  C  L  O  S
Y  M  S  Z  J  X  P  F  B  G  T  B  O  Z  P
H  O  O  T  E  R  S  O  U  B  P  S  D  A  H
B  P  S  G  U  J  O  Q  A  N  A  Q  E  B  C
M  U  W  L  A  B  W  P  Q  S  B  S  R  H  Z
P  P  K  Q  A  V  S  V  H  N  F  A  I  D  C
F  P  N  K  E  O  N  P  L  O  I  H  G  F  U
Z  I  F  A  C  H  T  C  Y  X  X  E  K  S  O
B  E  L  J  T  P  R  T  Q  Z  R  K  X  X  C
T  S  F  C  H  B  V  R  N  W  J  P  L  L  X
```

BAPS	BAZOOMAS	BOOBIES
CHESTICLES	CHIMICHANGAS	FUN BAGS
HOOTERS	JUGS	PUPPIES

LUSH LINGERIE CROSSWORD

Across

2 More enticing than braces. (10)

5 Your "snake" might ladder this. (7)

6 More seductive than your usual nightdress. (8)

Down

1 It feels good to get this off your chest. (9)

3 This isn't just for medieval dress up. (6)

4 Australian word for flip-flop. (5)

What is *oculolinctus*?

a. The act of licking someone's ear for sexual pleasure

b. The act of licking someone's eye for sexual pleasure

c. The act of licking someone's toe for sexual pleasure

d. The act of licking someone's finger for sexual pleasure

ANAGRAMS

Rearrange these letters to reveal the ultimate
female pleasure centre:

BUN LOVE

BONK NUT PIT

BILLED OVERSOLD

SUPPLY ARSE

SEXY COCKTAILS WORD SEARCH

```
W  H  D  D  O  U  T  B  S  T  U  M  G  E  S
E  R  C  K  E  Y  D  W  S  F  B  G  R  C  K
R  O  L  A  J  E  I  O  Y  G  A  Q  R  N  R
C  Y  F  E  E  L  P  R  N  D  Y  E  D  E  N
S  A  J  Z  G  B  R  T  R  A  A  N  V  C  B
W  L  E  H  G  M  E  Q  H  M  W  I  V  B  F
O  F  R  C  I  C  V  H  I  R  R  G  D  C  Y
L  U  D  H  S  A  W  N  T  D  O  C  U  A  W
S  C  M  G  H  O  G  M  W  N  S  A  M  B  Y
G  K  G  L  O  O  Q  E  G  N  O  H  T  M  V
N  Y  X  W  R  C  R  T  Q  J  G  X  W  Y  A
O  C  O  G  L  C  J  L  U  R  Z  Z  E  K  D
L  O  A  P  S  I  B  N  S  J  A  S  I  S  K
M  S  L  E  G  S  P  R  E  A  D  E  R  X  F
M  E  L  P  P  I  N  Y  R  E  P  P  I  L  S
```

DEEP THROAT	LEG SPREADER	WOO WOO
ROYAL FUCK	SCREAMING ORGASM	SCREW DRIVER
SEX ON THE BEACH	SLIPPERY NIPPLE	LONG SLOW SCREW

WORD LADDER

Change DICK into BOOB by altering one letter at a time to make a new word on each step of the ladder:

D I C K

__ __ __ __

__ __ C __

C __ __ __

__ __ __ __

B O O B

ANAGRAMS

Put these letters in the right order to see girls take matters in to their own hands:

BARGAIN MUTTS

BACK FELINE THING

GIBBON RUFF

FIND DEED GIRL

DOT-TO-DOT

Join the dots to find
the mystery image!

RAUNCHY RIDDLER

Solve the clues to find the mystery word:

My first is in **BOLLOCKS** but not found in **SILKY**
My second is in **LABIA** and never in **MILKY**
My third is in **CLIMAX** but not seen in **CACK**
My fourth is in **CALL GIRL** but never in **BACK**
My fifth is in **SLIDE** and also in **SIGH**
My sixth is in **PLAYER** but not seen in **PLIED**
My seventh is in **CONDOM** and also in **NICK**
My eighth is in **ARSECRACK** as well as in **DICK**
My whole word, if you want to know it
Is the bit that hangs below a man's dick

KAMA SUTRA CROSSWORD

Across

1 Sail away to the land of bliss in this position. (4)

6 Who knew that buses could be so much fun? (6, 6)

Down

2 You reap what you sow with this move. (6)

3 Light the fires of romance. (6)

4 Release your endorphins, not your dorsal fins. (7)

5 You'll find this position quite ribbet-ing. (4)

WORD WHEEL

See how many words of three or more letters you can make, using each letter only once. Each word must use the central letter. Can you find a word that uses all of the letters?

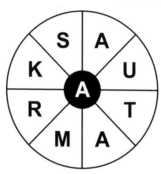

PAIRS

Can you match up the three sets of identical pairs?

BLOW JOBS WORD SEARCH

```
K K O Q K G L Y B R N W M K P
C E N Z H R I L V W G R B L F
I T J O C T O B O R Q Y A G E
D W C V B W H T A Y K Y I U L
G E K O J S N Q E C T L K D L
N Q V O G W L L K H E M O D A
I A B R O L R O E H U R T F T
K X U D Y A N P B K G D D O I
C W O G I V I N G H E A D I O
U G W Z F N O R G E M Q I M F
S B O N K E H T H S I L O P P
G N A O U G D O G Z Z G S A W
A S B Q M Y V V K Q I P I O B
K O H O H A T Y J K D M Z D I
E V G V C E O Y Q D E U Q Z M
```

BLOW JOB

DOME

FELLATIO

GIVING HEAD

GO DOWNTOWN

KNOB SLOB

PLAY THE PINK
OBOE

POLISH THE
KNOB

SUCKING DICK

DOT-TO-DOT

Join the dots to find the mystery image!

MISSING WORDS

Fill in the blank space to make two compound words or phrases:

Sugar		Cool
Butt		Socket
Role		Wright
Heavy		Zoo

IRRESISTIBLE INNUENDOS WORD SEARCH

```
D  W  X  T  D  L  T  U  S  E  O  T  D  F  B
A  U  B  E  R  G  I  N  E  E  M  O  J  I  A
M  E  L  C  I  S  P  O  P  E  I  O  H  S  N
T  A  E  E  A  E  Y  T  G  G  L  E  T  G  A
M  C  K  B  G  R  J  O  U  A  K  T  N  D  N
T  U  W  I  R  A  U  R  S  K  S  A  Y  O  A
J  O  F  E  N  Y  S  H  P  C  H  E  H  I  B
D  S  H  F  Z  G  O  U  I  A  A  M  I  Q  T
L  C  V  E  I  E  B  Q  A  P  K  X  N  W  A
Q  P  U  O  S  N  X  A  C  S  E  N  O  W  U
M  I  Q  I  E  D  Z  A  C  G  J  O  Z  F  L
J  M  Z  B  E  A  V  E  R  O  D  P  Z  C  O
N  E  W  Q  W  M  W  L  G  A  N  E  R  X  D
D  K  I  K  W  Y  Z  V  K  U  Y  R  F  R  S
N  N  P  Q  S  N  U  B  S  G  R  E  C  B  N
```

AUBERGINE EMOJI	BANANA	BEAVER
BONE	BUNS	CHERRY
MAKING BACON	MEAT	MILKSHAKE
MUFFIN	PACKAGE	POPSICLE
SAUSAGE	SHOE SIZE	WOOD

BOLD BDSM CROSSWORD

Across

3 You'll get sent here if you've been bad. (7)

5 There are seven levels of torture to this cock cage. (5, 2, 4)

6 Opens your legs and keeps them open! (8, 3)

Down

1 The patron saint would be shocked to find out what this religious symbol is used for. (2, 7, 5)

2 This will help you flay away the troubles of the day! (7)

4 Make sure your sub can't speak with this. (4, 3)

RAUNCHY RIDDLER

Solve the clues to find the mystery word:

My first is in **SMEAR** as well as in **TINGLES**
My second is in **REAMS** and also in **SINGLES**
My third is in **MANK** as well as in **MAG**
My fourth is in **SEX** but not seen in **SHAG**
My fifth is in **BUNS** but isn't in **BUM**
My whole word is a way of saying 'cum'

MAZE

Can you help Kelly find something that will satisfy her *sexual* appetite?

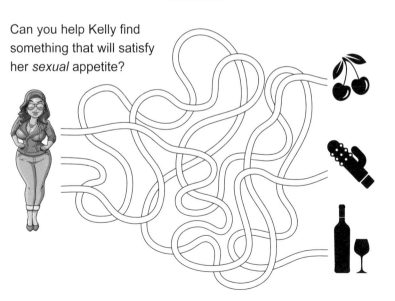

BOOTYLICIOUS BOTTOMS
WORD SEARCH

```
F  D  T  R  S  G  J  L  R  C  X  E  P  E  C
A  C  G  U  Y  B  U  C  E  A  X  Y  S  L  W
J  Q  Q  O  S  J  N  V  Q  U  Z  W  C  D  Q
T  S  P  H  I  H  K  L  F  N  E  Y  V  D  L
U  H  T  G  U  G  I  E  L  E  J  M  Y  A  E
T  O  V  K  B  B  N  E  T  H  M  U  X  S  V
X  R  F  A  U  R  T  C  O  M  G  C  O  Y  C
Q  S  F  K  X  T  H  X  G  Z  A  O  C  X  N
U  K  W  F  Z  E  E  L  E  R  B  G  E  E  C
U  X  Z  M  E  F  T  F  S  A  P  J  X  S  I
V  A  W  K  X  E  R  E  C  I  H  I  A  U  B
W  Q  S  K  H  R  U  K  E  I  S  T  E  R  O
K  N  O  D  A  K  N  O  D  A  B  F  Z  A  O
J  T  S  X  R  K  K  I  R  U  V  T  H  P  T
T  C  F  E  J  R  J  H  M  I  B  Q  J  Y  Y
```

ARSE	BADONK-A-DONK	BOOTY
CABOOSE	JUNK IN THE TRUNK	KEISTER
SEXY SADDLE	SWEET CHEEKS	TUSHIE

DOT-TO-DOT

Join the dots to find
the mystery image!

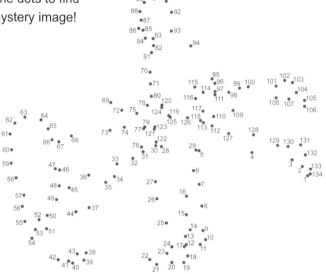

ANAGRAMS

Rearrange these letters to make words for boobs:

FAB SNUG

SOLEMN

EVIL POLL SOW

MAIM SMEAR

TRACKWORD

Find as many words as you can by moving from one square to the next in any direction, without going through any letter square again. Can you find the nine-letter word hidden in the square?

A	S	E
E	K	C
T	C	O

WORD LADDER

Change FUCK to BALL by altering one letter at a time to make a new word on each step of the ladder:

F U C K

_ _ _ _

_ _ L _

_ _ _ _

B A L L

BOUNCING BOOBIES CROSSWORD

Across

4 Also the name of a famous breastaurant. (7)

5 Where there are totties, there are ____. (7)

6 The most enjoyable carriers. (3, 4)

Down

1 Two adorable animals that live on your chest. (7)

2 Sweet, juicy, fleshy treats. (6)

3 Their primary purpose is for banging (on the door). (8)

Which of the following has more nerve endings than anything else in the human body?

a. The penis

b. The vagina

c. The testicles

d. The clitoris

DOT-TO-DOT

Join the dots to find the mystery image!

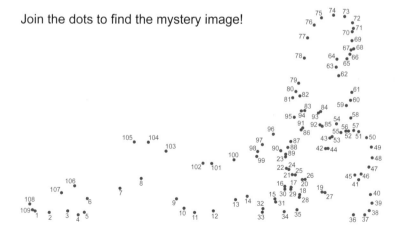

24

PAIRS

Can you match up the three sets of identical pairs?

WORD WHEEL

See how many words of three or more letters you can make, using each letter only once. Each word must use the central letter. Can you find a word that uses all of the letters?

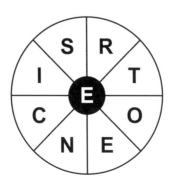

MISSING WORDS

Fill in the blank space to make two compound words or phrases:

Snow		Bag
Dip		Faced
Lady		Diver
Slippery		Tassel

RAUNCHY RIDDLER

Solve the clues to find the mystery word:

My first is in **ARSE** but not found in **DANCE**
My second is in **SCABBY** as well as in **CHANCE**
My third is in **RINGPIECE** but never **BUTTHOLE**
My fourth is in **CREAMING** but not seen in **GOAL**
My fifth is in **BAWDY** as well as in **WANK**
My sixth is in **PISSING** but not seen in **SORE**
My seventh is in **PENIS** but not found in **PUSSY**
My eighth is in **JUGS** and never in **JUICY**
My whole word is used to this effect:
A way of describing having sex

STUD MUFFINS WORD SEARCH

```
G  I  X  O  C  Q  C  Q  I  T  R  L  B  N  U
H  N  S  K  N  A  D  E  H  R  T  G  E  I  N
S  Q  I  B  F  L  S  P  B  E  X  L  E  F  F
S  R  N  M  I  K  L  A  M  R  J  D  F  F  Z
B  O  R  I  R  A  K  P  N  R  O  G  C  U  O
U  F  M  G  Y  A  T  R  E  O  M  G  A  M  W
B  G  R  B  R  N  H  L  L  P  V  V  K  D  Q
U  U  O  S  Q  U  L  C  X  I  H  A  E  U  N
R  Y  D  T  W  I  R  J  E  V  V  Y  P  T  G
D  E  N  T  K  H  D  V  Q  C  N  A  P  S  E
I  L  W  Y  B  C  M  F  Z  V  N  Z  W  T  M
E  A  D  L  H  L  H  S  K  L  K  I  M  T  T
L  A  Q  Z  E  X  G  M  Y  F  V  N  R  H  E
L  N  A  U  J  N  O  D  Y  Q  C  Y  U  P  Z
T  L  H  F  G  B  I  G  D  A  D  D  Y  H  M
```

BEEF CAKE	BIG DADDY	CASANOVA
DON JUAN	HUNK	LADY KILLER
PLAYBOY	PRINCE CHARMING	STUD MUFFIN

BOINKIN' BOOKS AND MUCKY MAGS CROSSWORD

Across

5 This bunny is a real page-turner. (7)

6 Saucy action with gardener got this book banned. (4, 11, 5)

Down

1 Animal rights groups wouldn't approve of this love godddess's outfit. (5, 2, 4)

2 It's a beautiful day in France. (5, 2, 4)

3 Smaller than Lady Garden Mountain. (5, 4)

4 The famous sex bible. (4, 5)

DOT-TO-DOT

Join the dots to find the
mystery image!

WORD LADDER

Change SHAG to CRAP by altering one letter at a time
to make a new word on each step of the ladder:

S H A G

— — — —

_ **L** _ _

— — — —

C R A P

FAMILY JEWELS WORD SEARCH

```
H V Q Y B C S X G T Y T R V S
Q X U A X O Z D S K A N K G L
C M V X D Z L D A Y A O N N E
Y I W E T X U L L N W N A C W
S S E W I P E H O K O M C V E
C K C A S T U N Q C T G K H J
Z L B E G V Z S Z B K Z E Y Y
A W V H N X I M A K A S R A L
S O G Z Q E J L Y L G D S X I
L Y E U L N L S P V W I E R M
Z H V V H B D U N T N Z L U A
E U O V A Q E N T P B S T D F
A H W G C C O I N P U R S E F
W X T U O S S O U N C I D C X
O U I V H N P Y D G N W R I W
```

BALLBAG	BOLLOCKS	COIN PURSE
FAMILY JEWELS	GONADS	KNACKERS
LOVE SPUDS	NUTSACK	TWO VEG

ANAGRAMS

Rearrange the letters to make sex positions:

O PROG LINT

HER WAR ELBOW

SEXY IN TIN

PING SOON

RAUNCHY RIDDLER

Solve the clues to find the mystery word:

My first is in **FISTING** as well as in **FARTS**
My second is in **EUNUCHS** but not found in **SEXY**
My third is in **TICKLE** but not found in **FINGER**
My fourth is in **DRINKING** but never in **WINE**
My fifth is in **STUD** as well as in **TITS**
My sixth is in **BANGING** but not found in **GITS**
My seventh is in **ROLE PLAY** but not found in **HOLE**
My eighth is in **WOOD** but never in **POLE**
My whole word, put all eight together and see
Is a word for someone who acts stupidly

MAZE

Can you help Jason find the fittest guy at his gym?

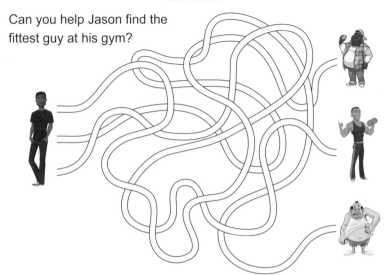

PAIRS

Can you match up the three sets of identical pairs?

MISSING WORDS

Fill in the blank space to make two compound words or phrases:

Motor		Load
Third		Camp
Sixty		Lives
Suck		Shore

SEX TOYS SUDOKU

Complete the following grid by filling in the empty
boxes with the missing icons. Each icon can
only appear once in a row, column or box

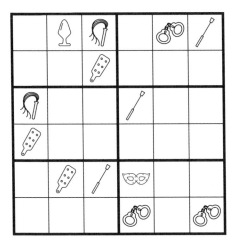

PERFECT PUBES CROSSWORD

Across

2 You might need to hire a gardener to trim this foliage. (4)

6 You can also put your hands in it to keep warm. (4)

7 Guides your aircraft home. (7, 5)

Down

1 The opposite of long 'n' straighties! (5, 1, 7)

3 You can always tell when this creature has been in your garden. (5, 5)

4 An exotic location south of the equator. (9)

5 Does it match the drapes? (6)

PAIRS

Can you match up the three sets of identical pairs?

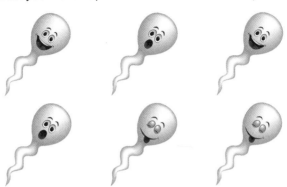

WORD WHEEL

See how many words of three or more letters you can make, using each letter only once. Each word must use the central letter. Can you find a word that uses all of the letters?

RAUNCHY RIDDLER

Solve the clues to find the mystery word:

My first is in **SUCKLES** but not found in **UGLY**
My second is in **PERVERT** as well as in **HERPES**
My third is in **STARFISH** but not found in **ARSE**
My fourth is in **GRUNTING** but never in **GRASS**
My fifth is in **RINGPIECE** but not found in **PISS**
My sixth is in **DILDO** but never in **DISS**
My seventh is in **LABIA** as well as in **LAME**
My eighth is in **SKANKY** and not found in **CAME**
My ninth is in **TOYS**, you won't find it in **BOYS**
My whole word's a way to say three is more fun

DOT-TO-DOT

Join the dots to find the mystery image!

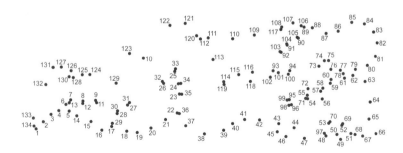

TITILLATING TOYS WORD SEARCH

```
E V T Q V U N N H Y K W C C S
B D K G A G O A J R E S A T P
U K W H H P N I N M O H N N Y
C Z W H A D G I E P A A D L A
E B A R C D I L D O P K Y F C
C W T U E M A O C S Y E G S Z
I S F P S S E O S J H D S T M
G F F E A T H E R D U S T E R
S N E F T I L G G Z V T R F Z
E S I K G H R O T A R B I V C
Y E T R C X H V N H M O N X R
U M X T K V H L Q U A O G T H
G W O X Z C J N K F M N A T A
K R K V S X O M G K A P P O G
C Z L L R A W C X K T A N N P
```

CANDY G-STRING	COCK RING	VIBRATOR
DILDO	FEATHER DUSTER	HANDCUFFS
ICE CUBE	STRAP-ON	CROTCHLESS PANTS

ANAGRAMS

Organize these mixed-up letters into ways to say "wanking":

JOCK FIG FAN

SHAVE SHADED LINK

ON OUR TUBE

A SLIM HEATSTROKE

WORD LADDER

Change BONER to HOLES by altering one letter at a time to make a new word on each step of the ladder:

B O N E R

— — — — —

— — S — —

— — — — —

— — — — —

H O L E S

OUTRAGEOUS OUTFITS CROSSWORD

Across

1 Santa could slip a treat into these. (9)

3 Thoroughly Scottish underwear. (9)

4 You don't have to wait until your wedding day to remove this with your teeth. (6)

5 Not your average stuffed toy. (5)

6 Wear this skin-tight outfit to make your partner purr. (7)

Down

2 Pussies you can slip your feet into. (6, 5)

Once inside a woman's body, how fast can an average sperm travel?

      a. 2 mph

      b. 5 mph

      c. 7 mph

      d. 10 mph

WORD WHEEL

Can you help Jane find the right translation for this German word?

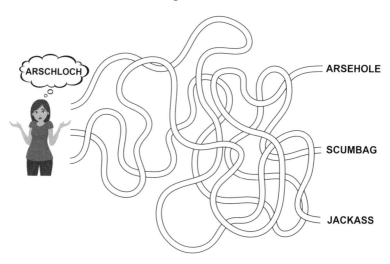

SAUCY SUDOKU

Complete the following grid by filling in the empty boxes with the missing icons. Each icon can only appear once in a row, column or box.

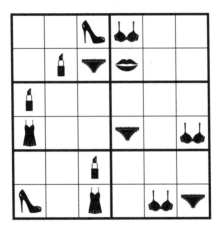

ANAGRAMS

Rearrange these letters to uncover some downright dirty drinks!

ADEPT OTHER

FLOUR YACK

DRAPERS GLEE

CLOWNS GLOWERS

WORD WHEEL

See how many words of three or more letters you can make, using each letter only once. Each word must use the central letter. Can you find a word that uses all of the letters?

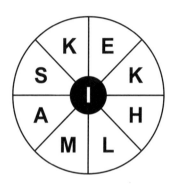

RAUNCHY RIDDLER

Solve the clues to find the mystery word:

My first is in **KNOBHEAD** but not found in **SLEAZE**
My second is in **LICKING** as well as in **PLEASE**
My third is in **CORNHOLE** but never in **CAME**
My fourth is in **WANKER** but not seen in **CLAIM**
My fifth is in **JUBBLIES** but not seen in **BOOBS**
My sixth is in **HOLE** as well as in **LOSE**
My seventh is in **BONER** and also in **BED**
My whole word is one way you can say 'give head'

JUST JISM WORD SEARCH

```
N  Q  B  E  N  M  C  L  W  N  D  J  J  I  C
R  N  U  P  S  S  N  O  I  Z  Z  Z  I  J  W
E  M  X  H  V  P  C  Y  U  Q  X  Z  T  B  B
T  M  K  X  J  I  O  Y  E  E  I  U  C  A  B
T  I  E  T  D  V  S  O  P  I  G  R  O  G  M
U  C  M  E  C  I  U  J  G  N  O  L  H  C  S
B  C  Q  O  L  F  W  Z  P  E  M  G  N  I  P
T  K  H  G  V  S  R  Y  U  A  M  Z  K  X  U
U  E  C  O  E  K  V  S  E  X  W  E  E  K  N
N  G  P  M  G  A  C  A  J  L  L  P  N  T  K
M  O  E  N  R  A  X  O  V  D  F  O  Q  Z  M
Q  N  S  G  Y  C  L  W  C  B  G  Y  Q  A  Q
Z  E  N  S  X  K  N  H  O  O  B  A  X  F  C
A  A  P  K  C  O  Y  W  N  G  Z  I  O  Z  L
M  M  U  L  A  Y  X  P  C  M  I  V  M  M  E
```

COCK VOMIT	JIZZ	MAN GRAVY
NUT BUTTER	SCHLONG JUICE	SEMEN
SEX WEE	SPOOGE	SPUNK

DIRTY DANCING CROSSWORD

Across

2 Firemen's favourite way to get frisky. (4, 5)

3 You need to get your weapon out for this one. (9)

4 Only do this if you can dance and undress at the same time. (5, 5)

6 You have to stay seated for this one. (3, 5)

Down

1 Instructions: impact your bodies together and abrade to completion. (4, 1, 5)

5 Tear up the dance floor with this carbonated orange beverage. (5)

DOT-TO-DOT

Join the dots to find
the mystery image!

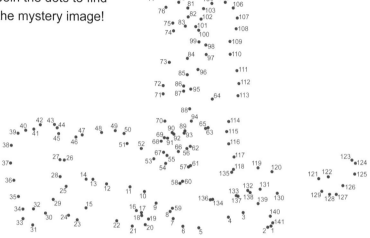

WORD LADDER

Change MINGE to WANGS by altering one letter at a time to
make a new word on each step of the ladder:

M I N G E

_ _ _ _ _

_ _ _ _ O

T _ _ _ _

_ _ _ _ _

W A N G S

TRACKWORD

Find as many words as you can by moving from one square to the next in any direction, without going through any letter square again. Can you find the nine-letter word hidden in the square?

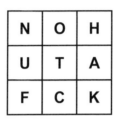

N	O	H
U	T	A
F	C	K

ANAGRAMS

Put these letters back in the right order to reveal a whole lot of ugliness!

BATHE THEE TWIN LUCKY GIST

MEN RIG

O SOME

CAT RUB FEET

SWEARING AROUND THE WORLD WORD SEARCH

```
S  N  I  Q  D  D  W  S  C  X  S  X  W  C  E
T  A  W  I  Y  Q  T  R  H  H  H  E  O  C  U
M  U  T  T  E  R  F  I  C  K  S  C  K  B  M
C  D  A  B  O  G  A  U  W  M  C  K  S  E  U
Z  G  C  N  A  F  N  K  J  A  H  H  S  R  Z
P  D  Z  X  F  S  U  D  K  M  E  S  Y  W  A
T  O  C  I  M  Z  T  J  W  V  I  F  D  G  U
H  I  U  E  I  U  W  A  S  P  S  T  Q  K  H
A  T  O  I  D  I  M  H  R  X  S  M  K  P  G
G  A  C  L  D  Z  G  Q  X  D  E  B  E  T  G
E  I  X  C  V  F  F  O  P  Q  O  V  K  E  H
E  N  R  U  A  H  Q  K  Y  J  V  O  P  D  M
N  M  Y  F  I  L  D  R  C  Y  M  O  C  R  I
Q  I  G  R  H  P  B  U  T  X  D  P  D  E  Q
T  S  K  F  T  E  T  A  S  V  E  E  Q  M  V
```

ARSCH   BASTARDO   IDIOTA

MERDE   MUTTERFICK   PISSE

SCHEISSE   STRONZO   TETAS

ANAGRAMS

Rearrange these letters to uncover some scintillating sex positions:

LONE BEARD

BIRTH EDGE

FLOOD THREATENING

RID THREE

SEXUALITIES SUDOKU

Complete the following grid by filling in the empty boxes with the missing icons. Each icon can only appear once in a row, column or box.

MAZE

Can you help Sienna find the person with the least clothes on?

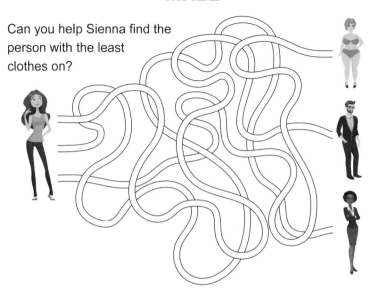

MISSING WORDS

Fill in the blank space to make two compound words or phrases:

Bubble		Lift
Stud		Top
Ball		Off
Bell		Game

FREAKY FETISHES CROSSWORD

Across

3 Better than a silver bath. (6, 6)

5 This kink is a bit squeaky. (6)

6 These kinksters give a whole new meaning to "doing it like animals". (5)

Down

1 Look at them go at it! (9)

2 Equestrians put on a show at the theatre. (4, 4)

4 Use your imagination! (4, 4)

WORD LADDER

Change WILLY to BULKY by altering one letter at a time
to make a new word on each step of the ladder:

W I L L Y

— — — — —

— — **L** — —

— — — — —

B U L K Y

MISSING WORDS

Fill in the blank space to make two compound words or phrases:

Long Slow		Driver
Dick		Fuck
Cock		Yours!
Kidney		Flicker

RAUNCHY RIDDLER

Solve the clues to find the mystery word:

My first is in **WATER SPORTS** but not found in **TROUSERS**
My second is in **CRAPPY** and never in **POWERS**
My third is in **INCHES** but never in **DICK**
My fourth is in **KINKY** as well as in **PRICK**
My fifth is in **WILLIES** but not found in **WEE**
My sixth is in **TUNNEL** but never in **GLEE**
My seventh is in **HUNG** but not seen in **HEALTH**
My whole word is for playing with yourself

DOT-TO-DOT

Join the dots to find
the mystery image!

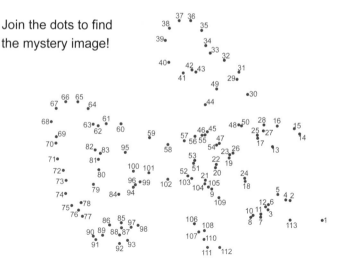

EXQUISITE ERECTIONS WORD SEARCH

```
Y E W E R V L V T D S V H Z K
F U L L M A S T E O M O Y M W
Y P S X T M A I K O W D K F E
M S M Y Q D X Z C W H Y L F D
I F Z F X G Q D O A V E R Y T
P E V K X R C J R X E I L N A
T F R N M I Z D H T A O F A Z
A H Q E U S O B S D I M T B P
R G L K C N L F E N W O E F Z
K L F I B T O B L E J E N Z T
R K E V R D I X F S M F T W T
X Q Q I O E Q O A X L T P U S
C V P R F W N C N M X H O Q S
Y F F I T S Y O W V Q Z L Z H
A S I T G I M I B N U S E D C
```

BONER

ERECTION

FLESH ROCKET

FULL MAST

HARD ON

ROD OF STEEL

STIFFY

TENT POLE

WOOD

ANAGRAMS

Rearrange these letters to reveal ways
to describe doing the dirty:

GANG SIGH

I DIG NOT

BEMUSE INSIST

BELGIUM SIGN UP

MAZE

Can you help Tom find
a right swipe?

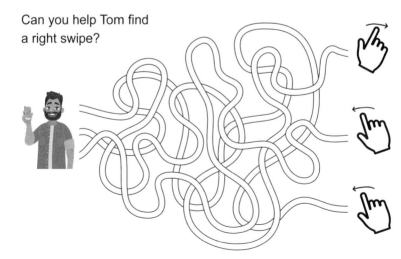

FRISKY FOOD CROSSWORD

Across

3 A light and airy dairy treat. (7, 5)

4 Helping people get jiggy since the Aztecs. (9)

7 Flame-haired, red-headed. (6)

Down

1 Not just for eating while watching tennis. (12)

2 Tasty on its own but perfect in a split. (6)

5 Drizzle this and get busy as bees. (5)

6 Shuck the shell and let it slide down your throat. (7)

ANAGRAMS

Rearrange these letters to reveal ways to describe the Big O:

EMPTIER TOTAL

CAME RIPE

LAC MIX

QUIT RINGS

SEDUCTIVE SUDOKU

Complete the following grid by filling in the empty boxes with the missing icons. Each icon can only appear once in a row, column or box.

WORD WHEEL

See how many words of three or more letters you can make, using each letter only once. Each word must use the central letter. Can you find a word that uses all of the letters?

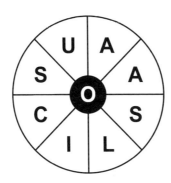

WORD LADDER

Change SHIT into BLOW by altering one letter at a time to make a new word on each step of the ladder:

S H I T

_ _ _ _

_ _ O _

_ _ _ _

B L O W

BONKING WORD SEARCH

```
O  B  U  M  P  I  N  G  U  G  L  I  E  S  N
M  G  W  W  L  G  R  R  U  E  F  M  H  G  O
E  B  N  W  J  F  U  B  C  K  J  A  J  B  P
A  H  U  A  T  V  J  F  N  L  B  L  M  Y  A
T  C  U  Z  T  L  Y  K  N  O  B  A  H  P  N
I  T  G  G  I  L  P  P  P  G  M  S  H  H  T
N  J  P  M  L  A  A  S  I  T  R  E  L  J  S
J  V  X  Q  D  P  N  T  T  L  E  H  P  O  D
E  M  Z  L  I  O  X  U  N  Q  H  T  B  G  A
C  I  F  S  I  C  B  F  U  O  C  E  G  R  N
T  B  P  Z  V  E  O  H  H  Z  Z  D  I  U  C
I  Q  R  H  R  V  S  E  O  P  J  I  D  V  E
O  G  G  A  O  H  S  P  R  A  K  H  R  R  I
N  V  B  Y  A  F  L  N  X  H  K  K  O  O  B
L  O  N  G  S  L  O  W  S  C  R  E  W  H  H
```

MEAT INJECTION   BONK   BUMPING UGLIES

HIDE THE SALAMI   HORIZONTAL   LONG SLOW
                          TANGO   SCREW

BARE BUTT   NO PANTS
MAMBO   DANCE   SHAG

RAUNCHY RIDDLER

Solve the clues to find the mystery word:

My first is in **PERIOD** and also in **PENIS**
My second is in **ORAL** and not seen in **SHERBET**
My third is in **RODEO** as well as in **RIDES**
My fourth is in **MINGE** and never in **SLIDES**
My fifth is in **CUMSHOT** but not seen in **SPLAT**
My sixth is in **TONGUING** but not found in **SHAT**
My seventh is in **ARSEFUCK** and also **RETENTIVE**
My eighth is in **AVERAGE** but not in **INVENTIVE**
My ninth is in **POON** but never in **TUNA**
My tenth is in **SHIVER** but never in **MOONER**
My eleventh is in **PSYCHO** but not found in **SWATCH**
My whole word's a thing that all men love to watch

WORD LADDER

Change TURD into GOLD by altering one letter at a time
to make a new word on each step of the ladder:

T U R D

— — — —

_ **O** _ _

— — — —

G O L D

LUSTY LOCATIONS CROSSWORD

Across

4 The ideal place to get your engine revving. (3, 6)

6 Get steamy! (6)

Down

1 You'd better hope you don't run into the teddy bears' picnic. (5)

2 You might share a hot dog and some salty popcorn here. (4, 3)

3 The perfect opportunity to join the Mile High Club. (9, 8)

5 Get a good rocking motion going and you'll be flying high. (5)

DOT-TO-DOT

Join the dots to find the mystery image!

ANAGRAMS

Unjumble these letters to see how three's a crowd:

I GO MAN EATERS

HE MET EROS

UNDENIABLE PERT TOO

AS STRIP TO

WORD LADDER

Change RUDE into TITS by altering one letter at a time
to make a new word on each step of the ladder:

R U D E

_ _ _ _

_ _ _ S

_ I _ _

_ _ _ _

T I T S

TRACKWORD

Find as many words as you can by moving from one square to
the next in any direction, without going through any letter square
again. Can you find the nine-letter word hidden in the square?

E	V	I
R	F	D
M	U	F

SEXY SPOTS WORD SEARCH

```
K J J O Z M Q L O D Q U V E H
V I F C W X U H A Z X Z N H C
L O T I N K Y L Q M F I U O A
J L D C Z Q L R K Y H N X T E
L E W A H E T Y M C T F D E B
B M M G Y E M K A G K R D L H
S V M W C B N M R V V F J R Y
K X A P V L G F B E M L Z O O
W Y R K X N A X L W W S O O T
F Y C N I Y D U F O U O T M L
O X H H O P E X Z X O S H X G
E U S T A E S K C A B R H S E
N A Z K E Q G Z R V T K Z M N
W H W N R E F M R P C R V H W
P U B L I C B A T H R O O M J
```

ALLEYWAY   BACK SEAT   BEACH

BED   HOTEL ROOM   KITCHEN FLOOR

PUBLIC
BATHROOM   SHOWER   WASHING
                                  MACHINE

63

ANAGRAMS

Unscramble these letters to uncover some popular manscaping techniques:

MOUTH TEACHES

IBIZA ONLY

CHINCHILLA PEAR

DARLING PINTS

MAZE

Can you help Olivia find the skimpiest pair of pants for her date this evening?

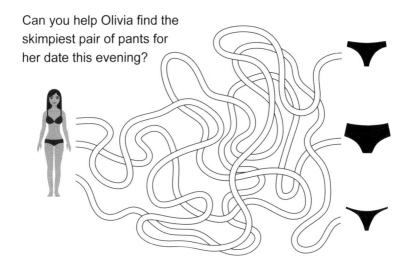

WORD WHEEL

See how many words of three or more letters you can make, using each letter only once. Each word must use the central letter. Can you find a word that uses all of the letters?

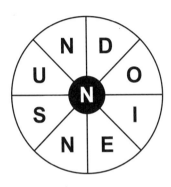

REBUS PUZZLE

Each rebus puzzle box below portrays a common word or phrase. Can you guess what it is?

♥ sight ♥ sight sight sight	**WEAR** **SEXY**	**LOLUCKYVE**

FRISKY FOOD WORD SEARCH

```
E  Y  K  P  Y  N  W  L  U  X  V  H  J  F  F
Q  C  E  D  R  T  P  X  U  K  M  S  M  E  F
T  I  U  N  I  Y  C  T  C  S  V  A  B  A  S
F  Z  O  A  O  O  I  W  P  D  E  A  I  W  E
R  R  Y  S  S  H  Z  R  Z  R  N  C  F  A  I
F  A  S  U  I  E  P  V  C  A  H  A  Z  O  R
P  S  T  K  A  C  T  D  N  H  P  H  F  M  R
I  M  E  C  T  E  E  A  D  A  T  G  V  I  E
U  P  R  P  W  P  W  C  L  P  I  U  B  D  B
J  V  S  Y  P  B  K  R  U  O  U  Q  N  X  W
M  R  O  I  Y  I  K  O  H  B  C  I  F  T  A
D  S  H  X  Q  P  U  R  Y  S  E  O  Y  J  R
W  W  C  U  C  U  M  B  E  R  B  S  H  R  T
C  D  F  X  R  R  A  L  I  E  O  B  J  C  S
W  D  J  H  S  D  J  W  Q  N  R  P  L  E  O
```

BANANA	CHOCOLATE SAUCE	CUCUMBER
HONEY	ICE CUBES	OYSTERS
STRAWBERRIES	SYRUP	WHIPPED CREAM

MAZE

Can you help Tom find the right translation for this French word?

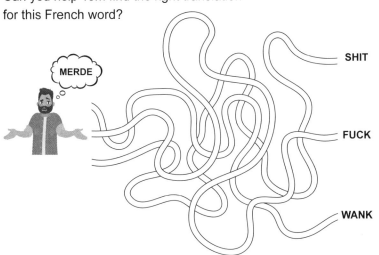

ANAGRAMS

Put in the right order, these letters make names for back-door fun!

BORN FED HIM

RUBY EGG

SUBTEXT

THE EAR SIN

DOT-TO-DOT

Join the dots to find
the mystery image!

WORD LADDER

Change DONG into VIBE by altering one letter at a time
to make a new word on each step of the ladder:

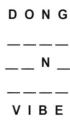

D O N G

_ _ _ _

_ _ N _

_ _ _ _

V I B E

MUFFS CROSSWORD

Across

4 This shellfish hasn't shaved in a while. (7, 4)

5 It might take a sensitive nose to sniff out this natural delight. (4, 7)

6 This isn't just a ride at the fairground. (4, 6)

Down

1 Some might say this is where the magic happens. (7, 6)

2 This red fish is most commonly found down south. (7)

3 Put your pilot here! (7)

PAIRS

Can you match up the three sets of identical pairs?

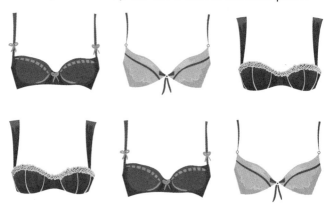

RAUNCHY RIDDLER

Solve the clues to find the mystery word:

My first is in **WANKER** but never in **CRANE**
My second is in **SHIT** as well as in **TRAIN**
My third is in **BALLBAG** but not seen in **BARGE**
My fourth is in **FLANGE** and also in **LARGE**
My fifth is in **DILDO** but not seen in **LARD**
My sixth is in **BEAVER** but never in **BARD**
My seventh is in **BOLLOCKS** but never in **BLOCK**
My whole is a word used for more than one cock

PROMISCUOUS POSITIONS
WORD SEARCH

```
L O I F T E Y S G D I T M B E
A R E P P I D G I B N R I J L
F C I H L M T D V A W K S A P
Y J G G I L V G R L Z B S U P
C W I P W Q R D F E A H I U I
X G H R X O Y Y B L T M O F N
S T C E V H C S L O J C N W Y
N S P R E A D E A G L E A R R
Z C H R H L R Y S Q V B R W E
E P I D B I B U G R N K Y J P
B F Q L N E P A Y G E V M W P
B G E A C W P B R V O V Q R I
C J F K Q R P L E R K D E R L
S E G E M E L B M I O T Z R S
K X L A N G O R V V Q W G A T
```

BALLERINA	BIG DIPPER	DOGGY
FIRE HYDRANT	MISSIONARY	REVERSE COWGIRL
SLIPPERY NIPPLE	SPREAD EAGLE	WHEELBARROW

During 30 minutes of active sex, the average person burns approximately how many calories?

      a. 100 calories

      b. 200 calories

      c. 300 calories

      d. 350 calories

ANAGRAMS

Rearrange these letters to reveal four favoured fetishes:

FIG MILN

ALLEY PRO

HORNLESS WODGE

PINK SNAG

WORD WHEEL

See how many words of three or more letters you can make, using each letter only once. Each word must use the central letter. Can you find a word that uses all of the letters?

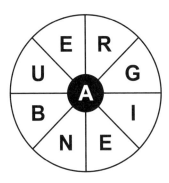

WORD LADDER

Change WINK into BANG by altering one letter at a time to make a new word on each step of the ladder:

W I N K

— — — —

— — — G

— — — —

B A N G

73

MISSING WORDS

Fill in the blank space to make two compound words or phrases:

Bed		Lid
Toilet		Mache
Waste		Line
Sewer		Out

RAUNCHY RIDDLER

Solve the clues to find the mystery word:

My first is in **BONK** but never in **WANK**
My second is in **OGLE** but not in **LINGER**
My third is in **PORNO** as well as in **DONG**
My fourth is in **SCABBY** but not seen in **SCHLONG**
My fifth is in **MINGE** and also in **FLING**
My sixth is in **SHITHEAD** but not seen in **QUIM**
My seventh is in **SEXY** but isn't in **FOXY**
My whole word is used for multiple tits

OUTRAGEOUS ORAL CROSSWORD

Across

2 You'll gladly offer this body part. (4, 4)

4 Easier than going up on. (2, 4, 2)

5 Instead of dining in tonight you could ____ ____. (3, 3)

6 More fun than sea snorkelling. (4, 6)

Down

1 Mix the dressing with the greens. (5, 8)

3 Many people enjoy their exhaling profession. (4, 3)

75

WANKING WORD SEARCH

```
G  N  I  K  N  A  W  Y  W  V  D  E  H  H  S
T  S  L  A  P  T  H  E  S  A  L  A  M  I  P
P  R  Q  O  U  K  N  K  E  X  E  Y  A  F  A
C  H  O  K  E  T  H  E  C  H  I  C  K  E  N
Y  C  R  U  Z  E  Y  M  K  N  I  D  C  J  K
P  W  R  W  S  N  W  K  E  A  G  A  J  A  T
C  E  Y  A  R  E  V  E  X  N  R  T  Y  C  H
E  C  I  T  C  A  R  P  E  L  F  I  R  K  E
C  T  F  R  Z  K  T  S  H  M  N  U  C  O  M
Q  O  K  K  P  O  O  I  N  F  U  C  A  F  O
T  O  V  W  S  L  F  N  Y  O  R  U  D  F  N
T  X  O  S  S  P  R  M  E  P  O  G  D  B  K
D  D  O  G  P  E  F  N  O  O  E  K  V  G  E
D  F  I  W  W  D  C  L  O  Y  F  D  E  I  Y
F  H  Y  B  C  R  A  Y  D  T  O  F  R  R  I
```

TOSS OFF	CRACK ONE OFF	JACK OFF
RIFLE PRACTICE	SLAP THE SALAMI	SPANK THE MONKEY
CHOKE THE CHICKEN	TROUSER SNOOKER	WANKING

DOT-TO-DOT

Join the dots to find the mystery image!

ANAGRAMS

Rearrange these letters to make words for jism:

A BARB BETTY

MY RAG VAN

GOD SLOPE

A LACE JUTE

WORD LADDER

Change BUTT into PEST by altering one letter at a time
to make a new word on each step of the ladder:

B U T T

— — — —

— — — —

— — — —

P E S T

RAUNCHY RIDDLER

Solve the clues to find the mystery word:

My first is in **CLITORAL** as well as in **CLUNGE**
My second is in **GONAD** but not found in **HUNG**
My third is in **WIFE** but not found in **GIRL**
My fourth is in **WANG** and never in **WANK**
My fifth is in **SICK** as well as in **SLIDY**
My sixth is in **CRAP** and also in **GRIMY**
My seventh is in **SNAIL** but not seen in **SIN**
My whole word is a position to have sex in

SCREAMING ORGASMS CROSSWORD

Across

4 A man spurts and a lady ____? (7)

6 Crack a pistachio. (4, 1, 3)

Down

1 A rocket goes off with a ____. (5)

2 Definition: the greatest point of intensity in a narrative or drama. (6)

3 He ____, he scores. (6)

5 A large vowel. (3, 3, 1)

REBUS PUZZLE

Each rebus puzzle box below portrays a common word or phrase. Can you guess what it is?

bidden bidden bidden bidden	ten tions **CRUEL** ten tions	A L W A **MY SIDE** Y S

REBUS PUZZLE

Identify the picture in each box and put them together to uncover some dirty words or phrases.

PASSIONATE POSITIONS CROSSWORD

Across

5 Except there's no hidden dragon. (9, 5)

6 Get yourself to the rodeo. (7)

Down

1 Let your love blossom like this sacred flower. (5)

2 Some like it ruff. (5)

3 A cut above the rest. (8)

4 The suspension is unbearable. (6)

WORD WHEEL

See how many words of three or more letters you can make, using each letter only once. Each word must use the central letter. Can you find a word that uses all of the letters?

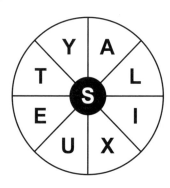

ANAGRAMS

Rearrange these letters to reveal words for lady parts:

DRAM DEBACLE

BE RAVE

PHONE TOY

LOON FLU EVENT

SERIOUSLY SHIT WORD SEARCH

```
Y  M  N  C  G  E  S  U  M  C  B  X  U  L  A
N  J  Y  N  O  T  C  W  P  P  Y  T  U  V  S
A  M  X  O  E  D  G  U  X  O  U  B  C  U  S
S  Q  O  A  U  T  E  K  E  R  Q  X  C  G  Q
W  I  M  V  O  X  L  B  S  D  H  T  H  K  U
Z  E  Q  W  G  W  E  D  R  D  K  T  T  N  A
R  W  A  O  L  F  U  A  D  O  F  A  Z  P  K
A  F  R  R  L  B  A  G  H  D  W  P  O  O  E
C  N  D  Z  Z  Y  X  N  Q  B  L  N  R  J  R
M  A  D  K  Q  Z  K  H  Z  D  H  U  N  W  O
Z  G  A  I  A  A  L  D  W  W  T  I  L  E  P
P  X  T  N  G  Z  G  O  W  U  I  X  E  A  H
H  I  E  I  K  O  O  D  G  H  H  W  R  U  H
K  Z  O  Z  Q  Q  U  X  J  H  S  C  M  C  E
T  O  V  F  I  I  J  L  J  A  Z  T  Z  S  M
```

ASSQUAKE	CODE BROWN	CRAP
DEUCE	DOOKIE	LOG
POO	SHIT	STEAMER

83

BUBBLE BUTTS CROSSWORD

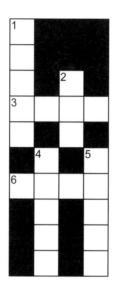

Across

3 Rhymes with bush. (4)

6 Bringing up the ____. (4)

Down

1 Pirates are particularly interested in this. (5)

2 Don't make a donkey out of yourself. (3)

4 Best enjoyed when soft and juicy. (5)

5 How much junk have you got in your ____? (5)

WORD LADDER

Change WANK into BONE by altering one letter at a time to
make a new word on each step of the ladder:

W A N K

— — — —

— — — D

— — — —

B O N E

DOT-TO-DOT

Join the dots to find
the mystery image!

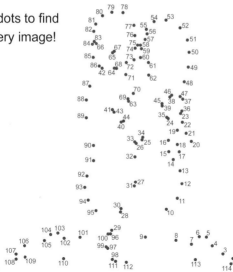

OBSCENE ORGIES WORD SEARCH

```
Z Y I X Z L T B E Y O E Z A D
G G L B O M A S F M S N N Y N
G R T H F N U D E U F L I D U
Q O E L D A O X O F B E S Y O
L O X C R W T H G Z G Y V I R
Z R A W W X D P H E J A D Y G
F M Q X F E B K K G N P H J Y
P U E P D H Y W P G J V C S A
Q T C W L O V E H U D D L E L
C E O K N U F P U O R G A X P
A R H A A Q A A U W D P P P E
C B V W Y T O R K H Y P V A V
U M G M L Z H R I J V N D R O
M D V T G J W O U T A Q Q T L
C S V L V K C N N Z Z N C Y Z
```

BAND CAMP   SEX PARTY   FUCKATHON

GROUP FUN   LOVE HUDDLE   LOVE
                                      PLAYGROUND

ORGY   CROWDED   SHAG FEST
                   HOUSE

86

ANAGRAMS

Put these letters back in the right order to reveal terms for todger:

MOROSE UTERUS

CARNAL DUTCH RUSE

SPACETIME LOP

DETER ENEMY SOON

TRACKWORD

Find as many words as you can by moving from one square to the next in any direction, without going through any letter square again. Can you find the nine-letter word hidden in the square?

T	I	S
F	A	H
D	E	C

ANAGRAMS

Unscramble these letters to uncover
some kinky Kama Sutra positions:

GLEE HEAT

CHAPLETS

EIGHT OCCURRING

BAPTIST BLOOMING

MAZE

Can you help Shanice
find a right swipe?

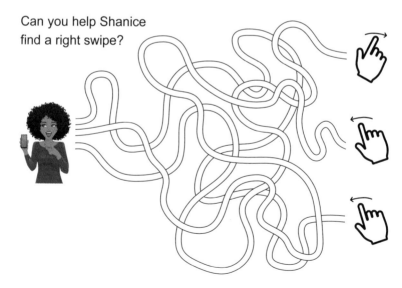

WORD WHEEL

See how many words of three or more letters you can make, using each letter only once. Each word must use the central letter. Can you find a word that uses all of the letters?

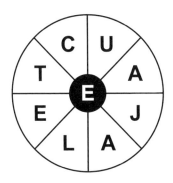

REBUS PUZZLE

Identify the picture in each box and put them together to uncover some dirty words or phrases.

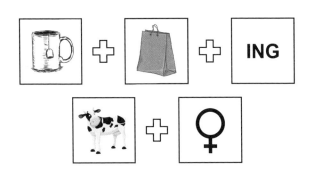

ANAGRAMS

Unscrambled, these letters are a load of balls!

SLOB LOCK

SCUM ROT

ANT SUCK

FLEE SLIMY JAW

In 2005 a sex toy was found, in the form of an eight-inch phallus. It is claimed to be the oldest of its kind, but how old is it?

a. 11,000 years old

b. 18,000 years old

c. 21,000 years old

d. 28,000 years old

RUMPY PUMPY CROSSWORD

Across

3 Also a deep-pile carpet. (4)

5 Get yourself some _____ and cranny. (6)

6 Also a comedy sound effect. (7)

Down

1 Your nose won't be the only thing getting blown tonight. (5, 5)

2 Give the dog a _____. (4)

4 A good go with a sausage. (7)

DOT-TO-DOT

Join the dots to find the mystery image!

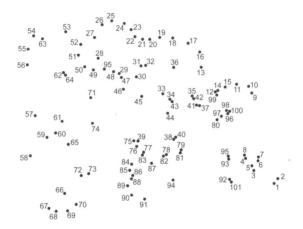

RAUNCHY RIDDLER

Solve the clues to find the mystery word:

My first is in **BONK** but never in **KINKY**
My second is in **ROUGH** but never in **ROWDY**
My third is in **TURTLEHEAD** as well as in **TITS**
My fourth is in **JOHN THOMAS** and also in **GITS**
My fifth is in **SLEAZY** but not found in **LUBE**
My sixth is in **LEERING** as well as in **TUBE**
My seventh is in **SEXUAL** but never in **SAUCY**
My whole word describes doing it in the arse

LOVELY LOVE TUNNELS WORD SEARCH

```
Z  L  E  A  J  B  Y  Q  D  F  B  C  E  V  Y
A  Y  O  G  Y  O  L  M  F  A  O  V  B  A  S
A  V  N  V  N  M  A  U  B  B  E  G  V  J  S
R  V  Y  W  E  I  M  O  J  E  C  I  P  A  U
H  K  N  W  I  T  M  B  L  E  D  U  A  Y  P
V  B  T  J  J  B  U  S  X  B  D  A  C  J  H
H  L  S  Z  E  R  S  N  D  K  E  U  A  A  G
D  H  L  A  K  D  N  Z  N  H  K  J  C  Y  F
D  X  V  P  R  N  W  C  C  E  W  O  W  O  O
N  E  C  A  R  U  D  L  I  K  L  C  U  D  Q
R  L  Z  N  P  M  N  R  D  X  M  N  R  M  O
E  I  G  J  I  V  Z  M  F  U  J  S  N  E  Q
W  B  E  A  R  D  E  D  C  L  A  M  T  F  R
K  X  P  K  V  D  Q  I  O  S  T  R  L  O  E
V  Z  H  B  E  M  E  G  N  A  L  F  L  Z  M
```

BEARDED CLAM	BEAVER	FLANGE
LOVE TUNNEL	MINGE	MUFF
PUSSY	VAJAYJAY	WIZARD'S SLEEVE

TALLYWHACKERS CROSSWORD

Across

5 This reptile likes to make his home in your apparel. (7, 5)

6 You keep this in your box. (4)

Down

1 Small, but with enough power to take you to the moon! (6, 6)

2 This fleshy musical instrument won't make a sound. (4, 5)

3 A move for rugby, football and the bedroom. (6)

4 A meaty anti-tank weapon. (4, 7)

RAUNCHY RIDDLER

Solve the clues to find the mystery word:

My first is in **FORNICATE** but never in **CRAVING**
My second is in **LONGING** but not found in **BATHING**
My third is in **BANGING** as well as in **ANGRY**
My fourth is in **COPULATE** but not in **STIMULATE**
My fifth is in **LANCE** as well as in **PRICK**
My sixth is in **FINGERS** and also in **DICKS**
My seventh is in **DOMINANT** but never in **TOP**
My whole word describes when a willy goes flop

PAIRS

Can you match up the three sets of identical pairs?

WORD WHEEL

See how many words of three or more letters you can make, using each letter only once. Each word must use the central letter. Can you find a word that uses all of the letters?

MAZE

Can you help Lin find the man with the smallest swimming trunks?

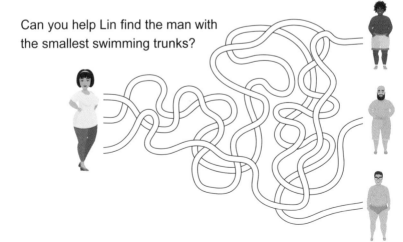

RAUNCHY RIDDLER

Solve the clues to find the mystery word:

My first is in **LOVER** but not found in **LONER**
My second is in **CLIT** as well as in **LABIA**
My third is in **BANGING** and also in **BONER**
My fourth is in **COCK RING** but never in **COPULATE**
My fifth is in **SHAFT** but not found in **SHIVER**
My sixth is in **TEASE** but not in **SEXY**
My seventh is in **ORGY** but not in **JUICY**
My eighth is **SCREW** but not in **BONE**
My whole word provides a lot of elation;
It's a great tool for sexual stimulation

What is *ithyphallophobia*?

a. Fear of seeing, thinking about or having an orgasm

b. Fear of seeing, thinking about or having an erect penis

c. Fear of seeing, thinking about or having a sexual encounter

d. Fear of seeing, thinking about or using a dildo

EJACULATIONS WORD SEARCH

S	E	H	Z	C	Z	P	Z	O	F	C	B	V	E	E
C	N	A	Z	W	F	O	Z	H	W	W	M	V	F	I
P	N	A	V	Z	Q	S	H	A	M	N	B	V	K	J
E	O	S	E	E	D	S	P	I	L	L	A	G	E	D
J	I	P	Y	J	S	W	H	Q	A	M	H	I	A	K
A	S	E	Y	N	R	N	P	S	M	C	U	O	M	V
C	O	Q	J	O	N	U	T	G	X	G	L	C	I	Y
U	L	W	I	H	U	O	O	R	D	R	L	G	X	A
L	P	H	L	G	F	R	M	Y	U	M	K	A	N	Q
A	X	O	Z	F	O	W	C	O	M	V	N	K	O	L
T	E	V	A	F	G	S	Y	O	A	A	R	V	F	Z
E	E	R	L	U	I	W	L	R	R	Q	E	K	S	T
E	V	P	U	U	O	C	W	H	P	K	C	R	R	N
K	O	P	U	L	P	B	A	R	T	L	T	A	C	M
E	L	D	B	Z	Z	I	J	L	O	H	A	M	V	P

BLAST OFF   POP YOUR CORK   SEED SPILLAGE

CUM   EJACULATE   JIZZ

LOVE EXPLOSION   BLOW YOUR LOAD   CREAM YOUR JEANS

ANAGRAMS

In the right order, these letters reveal terms for trimmed quims:

HASH VAN EVEN

LAZI BRAIN

GLAD PRINT SIN

OH DOLLY OW

WORD WHEEL

See how many words of three or more letters you can make, using each letter only once. Each word must use the central letter. Can you find a word that uses all of the letters?

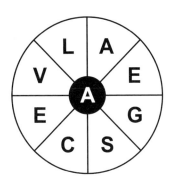

DOT-TO-DOT

Join the dots to find
the mystery image!

WORD LADDER

Change SUCKS into PANTS by altering one letter at a
time to make a new word on each step of the ladder:

S U C K S

_ _ _ _ _

_ _ C _ _

_ _ _ _ _

P A N T S

THROBBING THREESOMES CROSSWORD

Across

1 Rude behaviour at Sunday dinner. (4, 5)

3 Twice the fun, twice the misfortune. (6, 7)

4 More than two directions. (8)

5 Tourists love to climb this hard and pointy French landmark. (6, 5)

6 A triple French treat. (6, 1, 5)

Down

2 Help yourself to this snack of meat and two bread. (7, 8)

If you stroke, poke or tickle the nipple of a man or woman, how long – on average – will it take for it to go hard?

a. 2–3 seconds

b. 6–7 seconds

c. 10–11 seconds

d. 14–15 seconds

ANAGRAMS

Unjumble these letters to make rude phrases:

CHOKE BALD

A EURO SYRUP

HOT JAM NOSH

BUFF GORGE

LUSTFUL LITERATURE WORD SEARCH

```
U  S  F  H  W  R  X  R  A  S  L  L  B  N  J
A  N  O  R  D  H  M  R  O  U  H  L  E  P  W
A  T  N  N  L  U  T  F  S  N  B  I  L  J  G
G  N  A  I  S  U  O  T  T  S  T  H  L  Q  A
U  Y  V  R  S  A  F  D  S  Z  U  Y  E  N  A
X  T  U  A  T  U  N  S  G  O  Y  N  D  I  F
N  U  M  U  L  S  Z  D  Y  X  X  N  E  V  E
C  A  V  T  S  R  I  D  L  G  F  A  J  D  C
K  O  U  S  S  L  K  S  U  O  X  F  O  W  L
B  R  G  T  J  Z  P  Q  Y  E  V  E  U  J  H
K  J  U  S  T  I  N  E  P  L  X  E  R  I  M
C  N  J  N  O  V  V  S  V  V  O  G  R  B  Q
V  E  N  U  S  A  N  D  A  D  O  N  I  S  X
I  P  T  S  R  U  F  N  I  S  U  N  E  V  K
K  Y  J  Z  T  Z  I  H  K  M  M  B  B  M  Y
```

BELLE DE JOUR	FANNY HILL	JUSTINE
KAMA SUTRA	LUSTFUL TURK	LYSISTRATA
SONS AND LOVERS	VENUS AND ADONIS	VENUS IN FURS

SENSUAL SOUNDS CROSSWORD

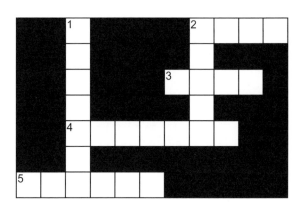

Across

2 For when you're taken by surprise. (4)

3 In pleasure, not in pain. (4)

4 The most appropriate sound for doggy style. (7)

5 ____ if you wanna go faster! (6)

Down

1 Good for sharing secrets. (7)

2 Also expressed when you are told a bad joke. (5)

DOT-TO-DOT

Join the dots to find the mystery image!

REBUS PUZZLE

Each rebus puzzle box below portrays a common
word or phrase. Can you guess what it is?

Head **Heels**	MILL**1**ION	**COLLAR** **100ºC**

PAIRS

Can you match up the three sets of identical pairs?

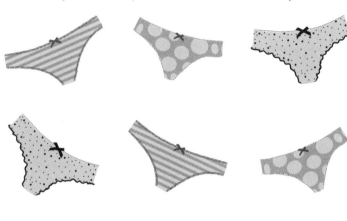

What is the record for the world's furthest ejaculation?

a. 10 feet, 4 inches

b. 14 feet, 6 inches

c. 18 feet, 9 inches

d. 20 feet, 2 inches

REALLY RANDY WORD SEARCH

I	L	Q	U	I	C	I	Z	B	C	W	Y	L	T	K
M	D	P	O	K	Q	Y	A	B	A	Z	R	U	H	E
P	V	E	Y	R	K	U	E	Z	V	A	R	F	X	E
A	P	N	S	S	L	J	I	G	K	N	B	T	W	N
S	E	J	I	U	A	I	V	P	E	H	C	S	F	R
S	M	R	N	H	O	S	V	D	E	I	P	U	K	H
I	F	Z	I	M	D	R	O	B	C	K	I	L	F	Y
O	G	O	E	I	I	N	A	G	V	N	T	B	E	G
N	H	O	R	N	Y	K	W	S	Y	T	W	Y	V	O
E	Y	G	P	P	I	Z	Y	C	N	U	U	W	I	E
D	N	M	K	H	I	T	U	C	G	R	G	V	Q	Y
N	H	Q	B	D	U	H	T	D	L	K	A	M	X	R
R	Y	U	L	I	K	Q	P	V	C	C	O	N	B	G
S	U	O	R	O	M	A	J	D	R	T	A	R	D	O
T	L	O	T	X	B	S	M	I	E	P	O	M	W	Y

AMOROUS	AROUSED	FRISKY
HORNY	IMPASSIONED	KEEN
LUSTFUL	RANDY	TURNED ON

MISSING WORDS

Fill in the blank space to make two compound words or phrases:

Big		Twister
Butt		On The Beach
Cock		Piece
Whipped		Pie

DOT-TO-DOT

Join the dots to find the mystery image!

108

WORD LADDER

Change BONG into HARD by altering one letter at a
time to make a new word on each step of the ladder:

B O N G

— — — —

— — **N** —

— — — —

H A R D

WORD WHEEL

See how many words of three or more letters you can make,
using each letter only once. Each word must use the central
letter. Can you find a word that uses all of the letters?

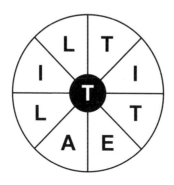

CRAP CROSSWORD

Across

1 Leave this to the gardeners. (4)

3 This sweet treat is always a hit at parties. (9, 4)

4 Take your refuse elsewhere. (4)

5 It may be big and brown but it isn't a tree trunk. (3)

Down

1 A word for a shit or a place you can sit. (5)

2 You'll wish we were referring to the ship deck. (4)

PAIRS

Can you match up the three sets of identical pairs?

How many sperm are there in the average ejaculation?

a. Up to 70,000

b. Up to 200 million

c. Up to 300 million

d. Up to 500 million

ANSWERS

p.4 Teasing Toys Crossword:
3. DILDO 6. SPANKING
PADDLE 1. COCK RING
2. BUTT PLUG 4. VIBRATOR
5. FEATHER

p.5 Maze:

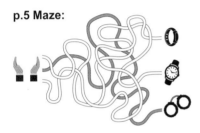

p.5 Word Ladder: TOSS – BOSS
– BASS – BASE – BABE

p.6 Dot-to-Dot:

p.6 Missing Words: RING, HOT,
DEEP, STRIP

**p.7 Beautiful Boobies
Word Search:**

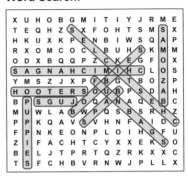

p.8 Lush Lingerie Crossword:
2. SUSPENDERS 5. HOSIERY
6. NEGLIGEE 1. BRASSIERE
3. CORSET 4. THONG

p.9 Trivia Question:
b. The act of licking someone's
eyeball for sexual pleasure

p.9 Anagrams: LOVE NUB, PINK
BUTTON, DEVIL'S DOORBELL,
PUSSY PEARL

p.10 Sexy Cocktails Word Search:

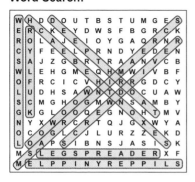

p.11 Word Ladder: DICK – DOCK – COCK – COOK – BOOK – BOOB

p.11 Anagrams:
MASTURBATING,
FLICKING THE BEAN,
RUBBING OFF, FINGER DIDDLE

p.12 Dot-to-Dot:

p.12 Raunchy Riddler:
BALLSACK

p.13 Kama Sutra Crossword:
1. SHIP 5. DOUBLE DECKER
2. PLOUGH 3. CANDLE
4. DOLPHIN 5. FROG

p.14 Word Wheel: KAMA SUTRA

p.14 Pairs:

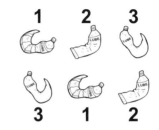

p.15 Blow Jobs Word Search:

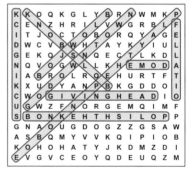

p.16 Dot-to-Dot:

p.19 Maze:

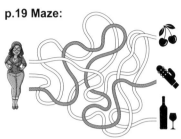

p.16 Missing Words: DADDY, PLUG, PLAY, PETTING

p.17 Irresistible Innuendos Word Search:

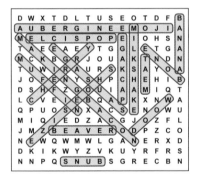

p.20 Bootylicious Bottoms Word Search:

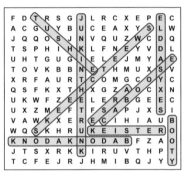

p.18 Bold BDSM Crossword:
3. DUNGEON 5. GATES OF HELL 6. SPREADER BAR
1. ST ANDREW'S CROSS
2. FLOGGER 4. BALL GAG

p.19 Raunchy Riddler: SEMEN

p.21 Dot-to-Dot:

p.21 Anagrams: FUNBAGS, MELONS, LOVE PILLOWS, MAMMARIES

p.22 Trackword: COCKTEASE

p.22 Word Ladder: FUCK – BUCK – BULK – BULL – BALL

p.23 Bouncing Boobies Crossword:
4. HOOTERS 5. TITTIES 6. FUN BAGS 1. PUPPIES 2. MELONS 3. KNOCKERS

p.24 Trivia Question: d. The clitoris (it has between 6,000 and 8,000 sensory endings)

p.24 Dot-to-Dot:

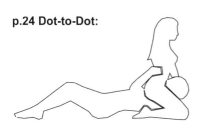

p.25 Pairs:

p.25 Word Wheel: ERECTIONS

p.26 Missing Words: BALL, SHIT, MUFF, NIPPLE

p.26 Raunchy Riddler: SCREWING

p.27 Stud Muffins Word Search:

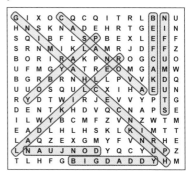

p.28 Bonkin' Books and Mucky Mags Crossword: 1. VENUS IN FURS 2. BELLE DE JOUR 3. FANNY HILL 4. KAMA SUTRA 5. PLAYBOY 6. LADY CHATTERLEY'S LOVER

p.29 Dot-to-Dot:

p.29 Word Ladder: SHAG – SLAG – SLAP – CLAP – CRAP

p.30 Family Jewels Word Search:

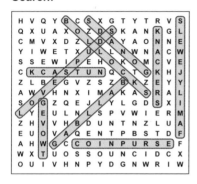

p.31 Anagrams: GIRL ON TOP, WHEELBARROW, SIXTY-NINE, SPOONING

p.31 Raunchy Riddler: FUCKTARD

p.32 Maze:

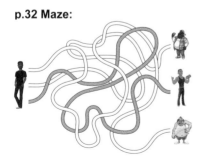

p.32 Pairs:

3 1 2

2 3 1

p.33 Missing Words: BOAT, BASE, NINE, OFF

p.33 Sex Toys Sudoku:

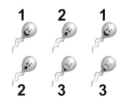

p.34 Perfect Pubes Crossword: 2. BUSH 6. MUFF 7. LANDING STRIP 1. SHORT 'N' CURLIES 3. SNAIL TRAIL 4. BRAZILIAN 5. CARPET

p.35 Pairs:

1 2 1

2 3 3

p.35 Word Wheel: SHAGATHON

p.36 Raunchy Riddler: SPITROAST

p.36 Dot-to-Dot:

p.37 Titillating Toys Word Search:

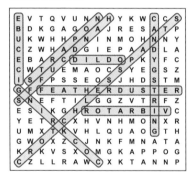

p.38 Anagrams: JACKING OFF, DEVIL'S HANDSHAKE, RUB ONE OUT, STROKE THE SALAMI

p.38 Word Ladder: BONER – LONER – LOSER – LOSES – HOSES – HOLES

p.39 Outrageous Outfits Crossword: 1. STOCKINGS 3. JOCKSTRAP 4. GARTER 5. TEDDY 6. CATSUIT 2. KITTEN HEELS

p.40 Trivia Question: d. 10 MPH

p.40 Maze:

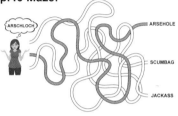

p.41 Saucy Sudoku:

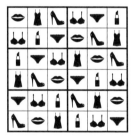

p.41 Anagrams: DEEP THROAT, ROYAL FUCK, LEG SPREADER, LONG SLOW SCREW

p.42 Word Wheel: MILKSHAKE

p.42 Raunchy Riddler: BLOWJOB

p.43 Just Jism Word Search:

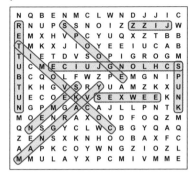

p.44 Dirty Dancing Crossword:
2. POLE DANCE
3. DAGGERING 4. STRIP TEASE
6. LAP DANCE
1. BUMP'N'GRIND 5. TANGO

p.45 Dot-to-Dot:

p.45 Word Ladder: MINGE –
MANGE – MANGO – TANGO –
TANGS – WANGS

p.46 Trackword: FUCKATHON

p.46 Anagrams: BEATEN WITH
THE UGLY STICK, MINGER,
MOOSE, BUTTERFACE

p.47 Swearing Around the World Word Search:

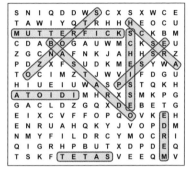

p.48 Anagrams: BANDOLEER,
THE BRIDGE, AFTERNOON
DELIGHT, THE RIDER

p.48 Sexualities Sudoku:

p.49 Maze:

p.49 Missing Words: BUTT, MUFFIN, SACK, END

p.50 Freaky Fetishes Crossword: 3. GOLDEN SHOWER 5. RUBBER 6. FURRY 1. VOYEURISM 2. PONY PLAY 4. ROLE PLAY

p.51 Word Ladder: WILLY – SILLY – SILKY – SULKY – BULKY

p.51 Missing Words: SCREW, HEAD, UP, BEAN

p.52 Raunchy Riddler: WANKING

p.52 Dot-to-Dot:

p.53 Exquisite Erections Word Search:

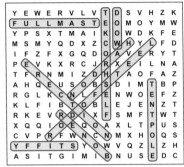

p.54 Anagrams: SHAGGING, DOING IT, BUSINESS TIME, BUMPING UGLIES

p.54 Maze:

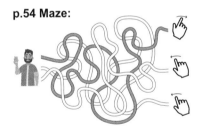

p.55 Frisky Food Crossword:
3. WHIPPED CREAM
4. CHOCOLATE 7. GINGER
1. STRAWBERRIES 2. BANANA
5. HONEY 6. OYSTERS

p.56 Anagrams: LA PETITE MORT, CREAM PIE, CLIMAX, SQUIRTING

p.56 Seductive Sudoku:

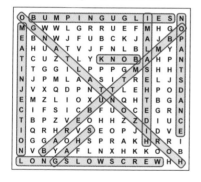

p.57 Word Wheel: SALACIOUS

p.57 Word Ladder: SHIT – SLIT – SLOT – SLOW – BLOW

p.58 Bonking Word Search:

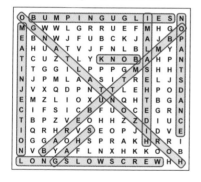

p.59 Raunchy Riddler:
PORNOGRAPHY

p.59 Word Ladder: TURD – CURD – CORD – COLD – GOLD

p.60 Lusty Locations Crossword:
4. CAR BONNET 6. SHOWER
1. WOODS 2. BACK ROW
3. AEROPLANE BATHROOM
5. SWING

p.61 Dot-to-Dot:

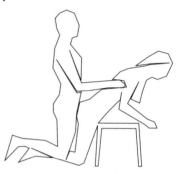

p.61 Anagrams: MENAGE A TROIS, THREESOME, DOUBLE PENETRATION, SPIT ROAST

p.62 Word Ladder: RUDE – RIDE – RIDS – RIPS – TIPS – TITS

p.62 Trackword: MUFFDIVER

p.63 Sexy Spots Word Search:

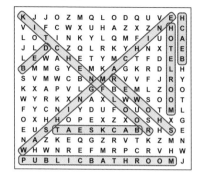

p.66 Frisky Food Word Search:

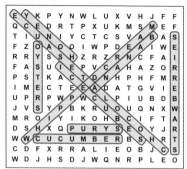

p.64 Anagrams: THE MOUSTACHE, BOYZILIAN, CHARLIE CHAPLIN, LANDING STRIP

p.67 Maze:

p.64 Maze:

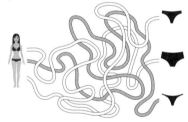

p.67 Anagrams: FROM BEHIND, BUGGERY, BUTTSEX, IN THE ARSE

p.68 Dot-to-Dot:

p.65 Word Wheel: INNUENDOS

p.65 Rebus Puzzle (from left to right): LOVE AT FIRST SIGHT, SEXY UNDERWEAR, LUCKY IN LOVE

p.68 Word Ladder: DONG – DONE – DINE – VINE – VIBE

p.69 Muffs Crossword:
4. BEARDED CLAM
5. PINK TRUFFLE 6. LOVE TUNNEL 1. WIZARD'S SLEEVE
2. SNAPPER 3. COCKPIT

p.70 Pairs:

p.70 Raunchy Riddler: WILLIES

p.71 Promiscuous Positions Word Search:

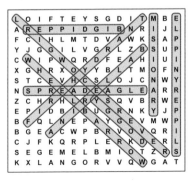

p.72 Trivia Question:
c. 100 calories

p.72 Anagrams: FILMING, ROLE PLAY, GOLDEN SHOWERS, SPANKING

p.73 Word Wheel: AUBERGINE

p.73 Word Ladder: WINK – WING – BING – BANG

p.74 Missing Words: PAN, PAPER, PIPE, RAT

p.74 Raunchy Riddler: BOOBIES

p.75 Outrageous Oral Crossword:
2. GIVE HEAD 4. GO DOWN ON
5. EAT OUT 6. MUFF DIVING
1. SALAD TOSSING
3. BLOW JOB

p.76 Wanking Word Search:

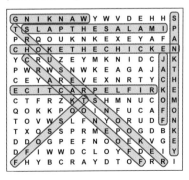

122

p.77 Dot-to-Dot:

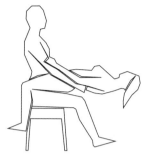

p.77 Anagrams: BABY BATTER, MAN GRAVY, SPLOODGE, EJACULATE

p.78 Word Ladder: BUTT – BUST – BEST – PEST

p.78 Raunchy Riddler: COWGIRL

p.79 Screaming Orgasms Crossword:
4. SQUIRTS 6. BUST A NUT
1. BLAST 2. CLIMAX
3. SHOOTS 5. THE BIG O

p.80 Rebus Puzzle (from left to right): FORBIDDEN, CRUEL INTENTIONS, ALWAYS BY MY SIDE

p.80 Rebus Puzzle (from top to bottom): CREAM PIE, FINGERING

p.81 Passionate Positions Crossword: 5. CROUCHING TIGER 6. COWGIRL 1. LOTUS 2. DOGGY 3. SCISSORS 4. BRIDGE

p.82 Word Wheel: SEXUALITY

p.82 Anagrams: BEARDED CLAM, BEAVER, HONEY POT, TUNNEL OF LOVE

p.83 Seriously Shit Word Search:

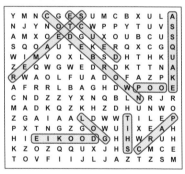

p.84 Bubble Butts Crossword:
3. TUSH 6. REAR 1. BOOTY
2. ASS 4. PEACH 5. TRUNK

p.85 Word Ladder: WANK – BANK – BAND – BANE – BONE

p.85 Dot-to-Dot:

p.86 Obscene Orgies Word Search:

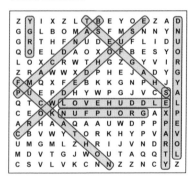

p.87 Anagrams: TROUSER MOUSE, CUSTARD LAUNCHER, MEAT POPSICLE, ONE EYED MONSTER

p.87 Trackword: SHITFACED

p.88 Anagrams: THE EAGLE, THE CLASP, CROUCHING TIGER, SPLITTING BAMBOO

p.88 Maze:

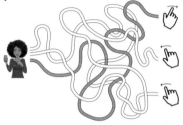

p.89 Word Wheel: EJACULATE

p.89 Rebus Puzzle (from top to bottom): TEABAGGING, COWGIRL

p.90 Anagrams: BOLLOCKS, SCROTUM, NUTSACK, FAMILY JEWELS

p.90 Trivia Question: d. 28,000 years old

p.91 Rumpy Pumpy Crossword:
3. SHAG 5. NOOKIE
6. BONKING 1. HANKY PANKY
2. BONE 4. PORKING

p.92 Dot-to-Dot:

p.92 Raunchy Riddler:
BUTTSEX

p.93 Lovely Love Tunnels Word Search:

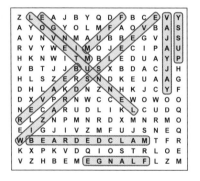

p.94 Tallywhackers Crossword:
5. TROUSER SNAKE 6. TOOL
1. POCKET ROCKET 2. SKIN
FLUTE 3. TACKLE 4. BEEF
BAZOOKA

p.95 Raunchy Riddler: FLACCID

p.95 Pairs:

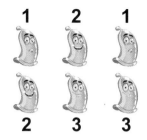

p.96 Word Wheel: FOREPLAY

p.96 Maze:

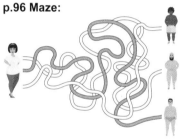

p.97 Raunchy Riddler:
VIBRATOR

p.97 Trivia Question: b. fear of seeing, thinking about or having an erect penis

p.98 Ejaculations Word Search:

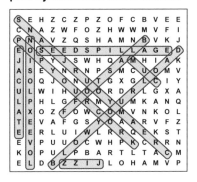

p.99 Anagrams: SHAVEN
HAVEN, BRAZILIAN, LANDING
STRIP, HOLLYWOOD

p.99 Word Wheel: CLEAVAGES

p.100 Dot-to-Dot:

p.100 Word Ladder: SUCKS
– SACKS – PACKS – PACTS –
PANTS

**p.101 Throbbing Threesomes
Crossword:** 1. SPIT ROAST
3. DOUBLE TROUBLE
4. THREEWAY 5. EIFFEL
TOWER 6. MÉNAGE A TROIS
2. SAUSAGE SANDWICH

p.102 Trivia Question: b. 6–7
seconds

p.102 Anagrams: BLOCKHEAD,
UP YOUR ARSE, JOHN
THOMAS, BUGGER OFF

**p.103 Lustful Literature
Word Search:**

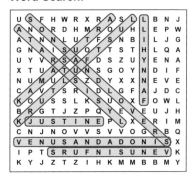

**p.104 Sensual Sounds
Crossword:**
2. GASP 3. MOAN 4. PANTING
5. SCREAM 1. WHISPER
2. GROAN

p.105 Dot-to-Dot:

p.105 Rebus Puzzle (from left to right): HEAD OVER HEELS, ONE IN A MILLION, HOT UNDER THE COLLAR

p.106 Pairs:

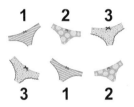

p.106 Trivia Question: c. 18 feet, 9 inches

p.107 Really Randy Word Search:

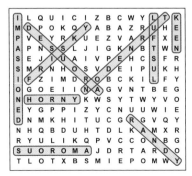

p.108 Missing Words: TITTY, SEX, RING, CREAM

p.108 Dot-to-Dot:

p.109 Word Ladder: BONG – BANG – HANG – HAND – HARD

p.109 Word Wheel: TITILLATE

p.110 Crap Crossword:
1. SOIL 3. CHOCOLATE CAKE
4. DUMP 5. LOG 1. STOOL
2. POOP

p.111 Pairs:

p.111 Trivia Question: c. up to 300 million

If you're interested in finding out more about our books,
find us on Facebook at **Summersdale Publishers**
and follow us on Twitter at **@Summersdale**.

www.summersdale.com

Image Credits